WHAT IF

there's hope for me?

A STUDY THROUGH GALATIANS AND EPHESIANS WITH

MIKE SILVA

*"If the Word of God isn't in you,
the world around you will consume you."*

MARK E. MOORE[1]

---

[1] Mark E. Moore, *CORE 52 Student Edition* (Colorado Springs: WaterBrook, 2021), 200.

"Faith is taking the first step even when you don't see the whole staircase."

MARTIN LUTHER KING JR.[2]

---

2 As quoted in "The lost speech and other words of Martin Luther King, Jr.,"
Glossophilia: The Love of Language, last modified January 16, 2017,
https://www.glossophilia.org/2017/01/the-lost-speech-and-other-words-of-martin-luther-king-jr/

Contents

Foreword

Why This Resource?

THE ISSUE OF BIBLE ENGAGEMENT

The last time I checked, the Bible had been translated into approximately 692 languages and was potentially available to over 5.6 billion of the world's 7.4 billion people.[3] Although the majority could reach for a copy of the Scriptures, the reality is "we" don't!

When Scripture is a driving force in a person's life, that person is influenced—mind, body, and soul—by the Word of God.

And how does Bible engagement manifest in a person's life? Barna researchers with the AG Bible Engagement Project[4] found that people who engaged with the Bible at least four times a week were 228% more likely to share their faith. They were 231% more likely to disciple others, 407% more likely to memorize Scripture, and three times as likely to volunteer in the **local church.**

Devotion to the Word of God also significantly strengthens the demonstration of the fruit of the Spirit in people's lives, increases life-satisfaction, and doubles the likelihood they will daily experience joy and peace.

RENEE GRIFFITH-GRANTHAM

---

[3] As of July 1, 2021, a more accurate number was 7.87 billion.
[4] To download the full report, visit bibleengagementproject.com/Barna.

Preface

Why this journal? Because it works! Listen to me—start your day with silence, or the noise of the world will silence the voice of God.

Silence takes practice but pays huge dividends!

"All of humanity's problems stem from man's inability to sit quietly in a room alone." ~Blaise Pascal[4]

I promise you will discover with this journal, "God speaks loudest when we're quietest."[5]

My vision is to:

Engage every believer with the Word of God, so that their intimacy with the Holy Spirit is their profound priority.

Inspire followers of Jesus that HE will speak when we listen intentionally for HIS voice.

Captivate Jesus-followers with this highly beneficial user-friendly transformational resource.

Enjoy, my friend, for the One who brought the Apostle Paul and me to our senses is about to do the same for you!

---

[5] From *Pensées,* as quoted at *Goodreads,* November 17, 2021,
https://www.goodreads.com/author/quotes/10994.Blaise_Pascal
[6] Mark Batterson, *Win the Day,* (CO: Multnomah Books, 2020), 188.

Acknowledgments

One of my friends and great mentors was the late Dr. Luis Palau. I remember hearing him share loud and proud about how great his team was! The message resonates in my heart even at this moment.

Therefore, to the team of all teams, I say thank you! Delight and Kristianna, without you, this project would have stalled, but with you, it lives. Thank you!

To editor Ruth Happ and designer Jaylen Fast, thank you for all your hard work and thoughtful feedback.

Thank you, team, for investing your heart, soul, and expertise in this great spiritual development tool.

How to Use This Journal

Answer three prompts every day: *So what? Now what? Here's what...* I love this. It is simple but highly effective. Use the Bible on the YouVersion App or whatever translation is available to you. I have included examples from my own reading, listening, reflection, and prayer; however, this is your journal! What you record here will live on as a legacy for those you love and all those who follow your example.

SO WHAT is God saying to me today?

This is where we listen!

Nothing is more important than what God says to YOU. He wants to speak to YOU. Pray this, "Lord, would you cleanse my heart? I confess my sins to you. Now, please speak to me as I read Your Word."

I guarantee He will.

NOW WHAT will I do?

This is action!

As you read, "God-thoughts" (ideas or promptings) will enter your mind. When they do, write them down.

Because of what God just said, what are you going to do? What action will you take?

HERE'S WHAT I pray...

This is our response!

I included a simple prayer as an example for you to write your own prayer. When God speaks to us, we want to do what He says. So, in your prayer, ask Him to help you do what He says.

The two books we are now studying were written to the cities of
Galatia and Ephesus, highlighted below!

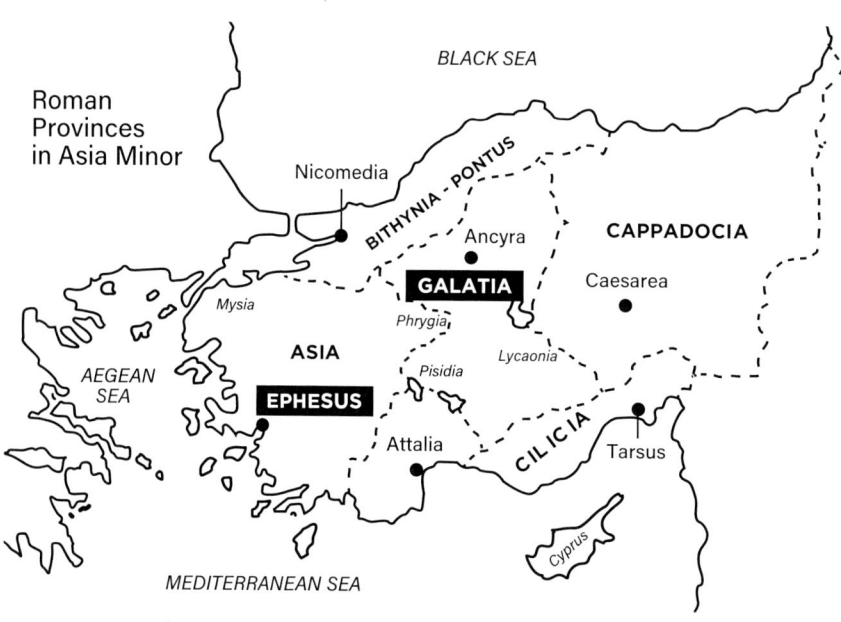

Context

GALATIANS

Paul writes Galatians to Jewish Christians who were straying from the Lord by relying once again on the works of the law of Moses. "The book reminds Jesus followers to embrace the Gospel message of the crucified Messiah, that justifies all people through faith alone, and empowers them to live like Jesus did."[6]

EPHESIANS

In the words of *Bible Project:*[7]

> In Paul's letter to the Ephesians, he speaks to Jews and non-Jews, two groups that were divided by so many factors it would have taken an act of God to unite them. In the first three chapters, Paul teaches about the great measures God took in order to make these two groups into one new humanity in Jesus. Then in the last three chapters, Paul shows them how Jesus' unifying work should impact every relationship and aspect of their lives.

---

[7]   "Galatians: Learn More," *Bible Project*, 2021, https://bibleproject.com/explore/video/galatians/
[8]   "Ephesians," *Bible Project*, 2021, https://bibleproject.com/church-at-home/week23-ephesians/

Galatians

Galatians 1:1–10

SO WHAT is God saying to me today?

1. These verses make the Gospel as clear as it gets. "Jesus gave His life for our sins, just as God our Father planned, in order to rescue us from this contaminated world in which we live."

2. Paul says, "I am shocked that [many of you] who committed to follow Christ are now turning away from Him." Therefore, I will heed Paul's advice to be aware of my surroundings, pay close attention to my "friends," and focus on the Word of God. Watch out for those who "twist" the truth.

3.

4.

5.

NOW WHAT will I do?

1. I will use God's Word the next time I share the Gospel message! My responsibility is not to "create" the message, just share it!

2. I will exhort followers of Christ, like Paul did. Stop! Repent! Come back into fellowship with Jesus and His church. Do not be tricked or drawn away by friends, culture, or my circumstances.

3.

4.

5.

HERE'S WHAT I pray...

Dearest Jesus,
thank You for giving Your life
to rescue me from this wicked world.
Thank You for allowing me to serve You.
I need no other acceptance but Yours alone!
May I spend my life not only announcing Your Good News,
but also exhorting believers to stay the course
and not drift, quit, or abandon You.
In Jesus' name. Amen!

Your prayer here...

ADDITIONAL NOTES

"Remember: God uses rescued people to rescue people."

CHRISTINE CAINE[8]

---

[9]   Christine Caine, Facebook, August 30, 2017.
https://www.facebook.com/143678730088/posts/10159388446265089/

Galatians 1:11–24

SO WHAT is God saying to me today?

1. *Before* (key word) Paul was born, God, in His grace, had chosen him to proclaim the gospel to the Gentiles! As it was true for Paul, it is true for me and you!

2. I do not need the approval of men. I need to be alone with God and receive my instruction from the Holy Spirit, then "go proclaim" what I'm given! Nothing else matters!

3.

4.

5.

NOW WHAT will I do?

1. I will intentionally get alone, be quiet, and listen to what the Holy Spirit wants to impart to me. Once I *get* a "word" from Him, I'm qualified to *share* with others—not before!

2. I will not quit, question, or doubt that I am doing what I was created and called to be and do!

3. I will strengthen myself in the Lord, knowing that intelligence, resource, or popularity does not qualify me to serve Jesus Christ—the Holy Spirit does. Period!

4.

5.

HERE'S WHAT I pray...

Holy Spirit,
I cry out for a word from You.
Give me ears to hear
what You want to say to me today!
And then, like Paul, may I proclaim it boldly!
 In Jesus' name, Amen!

Your prayer here...

ADDITIONAL NOTES

"The Good News is...
because of Jesus,
there is more to life!"

MIKE SILVA

READ

Galatians 2:1–21

SO WHAT is God saying to me today?

1. Just as God "directed" Paul, He will, through the Holy Spirit, lead me, as I seek Him and listen for His voice!

2. I must never quit helping the poor! As a priority since the beginning of the Church, this must be my passion and privilege.

3. A person is made right with God by faith in Jesus Christ. Nothing else! I cannot earn righteousness by obeying the Law. I am crucified with Christ, and therefore He lives in me. Period!

4.

5.

NOW WHAT will I do?

1. I will look for and listen to the Holy Spirit moving in my life. Expect it!

2. I will reflect on and memorize Gal. 2:10: "Keep on helping the poor."

3. I will remind myself it is no longer I who live, but Christ who lives in me, and I will daily choose to surrender control of my life to Him.

4.

5.

HERE'S WHAT I pray...

Blessed Holy Spirit,
I'm looking for You to direct every detail of my life.
I'm expecting You to speak to me; therefore, I listen.
My message is not my own; I simply "deliver" Yours!
Help me communicate with my words and my life
that "we are made right with God only by faith in Jesus Christ."
Nothing more, nothing else!
Lord Jesus, please, live *in* and *through* me!
In Your Holy name I pray, amen.

Your prayer here...

ADDITIONAL NOTES

Galatians 3:1–14

SO WHAT is God saying to me today?

1. We receive the Holy Spirit by faith when we believe the message about Jesus!

2. The "children of Abraham" are those who put their faith in God. We are made right and acceptable to God by faith in Christ alone! All who put their faith in Jesus share the *same* blessing Abraham received because of faith!

3.

4.

5.

NOW WHAT will I do?

1. I will thank my God that every spiritually good thing in my life comes to me by faith alone and the Lord's grace in my life.

2. I will be strengthened in my spirit today because Abraham's blessing is all mine by faith in Christ Jesus! This is significant for me because nobody was more blessed by God than Abraham.

3.

4.

5.

HERE'S WHAT I pray...

Oh, God of creation,
it's time for me to lift my heart, hands,
and attitude to You today.
Thank You for the gift of the Holy Spirit.
Thank You for the inheritance and authority
that are mine through faith in Christ alone!
Hallelujah! I bless Your name! Amen.

Your prayer here...

ADDITIONAL NOTES

*"Now faith is the substance of things hoped for,
the evidence of things not seen."*

HEBREWS 11:1 NKJV

Galatians 3:15-29

SO WHAT is God saying to me today?

1. We are all prisoners of sin. By believing in Jesus, however, freedom is my new reality! I am made right with God and adopted as a child of God by faith in Christ Jesus! And *that* is Good News to share with others!

2. I am a descendant of Abraham and, therefore, an heir of God's promise to him. Remember, the agreement God made with Abraham is irrevocable. God's promises are true and everlasting!

3.

4.

5.

NOW WHAT will I do?

1. I will praise God that I am no longer a prisoner of sin! Because of my belief in Jesus, I am free from the bondage of sin and condemnation.

2. I will carry this with me wherever I go, that I am a blessed son and heir of all God's promises!

3.

4.

5.

HERE'S WHAT I pray...

I praise You, Holy Spirit,
that I am no longer a prisoner of sin.
No more bondage for me.
The power of the shed blood of Jesus,
through my faith in Him, has set me free!
Thank You, Mighty and Gracious God.
Use me to stir Your people to love, honor,
and serve You in a greater capacity.
In the name of Jesus, my Bondage-Breaker,
Savior, and Promise-Keeper! Amen.

Your prayer here...

ADDITIONAL NOTES

"Never let the fear of striking out keep you from playing the game!"

BABE RUTH[9]

10   As quoted at Goodreads, accessed November 17, 2021,
      https://www.goodreads.com/quotes/304869-never-let-the-fear-of-striking-out-keep-you-from

Galatians 4:1–20

SO WHAT is God saying to me today?

1. It was at the perfect time God sent His Son Jesus to rescue and redeem us and to relate the plan of God to the world. Jesus came to purchase our freedom from the bondage of sin and death.

2. The God of all Creation set me free from sin and adopted me as His own child! And because I'm His child, He has made me His heir and sent the Holy Spirit into my heart, prompting me to call out, "Abba Father!"

3.

4.

5.

NOW WHAT will I do?

1. I will express my gratitude and praise to God the Father for the indescribable gift of His Son Jesus Christ. I do not express enough gratitude for the overwhelming gift of my Savior Jesus!

2. I will live with new confidence because the God of Abraham, Isaac, and Jacob has adopted me as His heir and sent His Holy Spirit to make His home in me! Therefore, I will choose to stop living discouraged about earthly situations. I am blessed and well-cared for. My future is bright and secure; I will keep my gaze fixed upward toward the matchless hope of Heaven and the reward of eternity with my Savior Jesus!

3.

4.

HERE'S WHAT I pray...

Jesus, You are the greatest gift
I *have* ever and *will* ever receive!
It seems like every day I read Your Word,
I see another "facet" of Your character.
I'm overwhelmed by Your grace.
When I think about being in relationship with You
because I'm an "heir," and having Your Spirit live within me,
I'm speechless. *Thank You for Your love.* Amen.

Your prayer here...

ADDITIONAL NOTES

"God never said that the journey would be easy, but He did say that the arrival would be worthwhile."

MAX LUCADO[10]

11 Max Lucado, *In the Eye of the Storm and the Applause of Heaven: Two Inspirational Classics in One Volume* (Nashville, TN: Thomas Nelson, 1995), page unknown, as quoted at https://www.goodreads.com/work/quotes/39841070-in-the-eye-of-the-storm-and-the-applause-of-heaven-two-inspirational-cla

Galatians 4:21–31

SO WHAT is God saying to me today?

1. I am an adopted son of promise, just like Isaac! As such, I receive the same multi-generational promised blessing God gave Abraham and Sarah!

2.

3.

4.

5.

NOW WHAT will I do?

1. I will thank my God for adopting me into His eternal and irresistible family. My course is set. My future, secure. My position, established. I am an heir of the Abrahamic covenant. I am a descendant of Abraham and Sarah.

2.

3.

4.

HERE'S WHAT I pray...

Great God in heaven,
giver of life and destinies,
thank You for adopting me into Your family.
Thank You for a "family tree" that begins
with my ancestors, Abraham and Sarah.
What a lineage!
What blessing and inheritance are mine,
coming from You, *through* them, *to* me.
How am I ever to thank You enough?
Who am I to receive a gift like this?
Lord God, I offer myself—all that I am—
in service to You, for all of my days. Amen.

Your prayer here...

ADDITIONAL NOTES

Galatians 5:1-26

SO WHAT is God saying to me today?

1. Christ has truly set us free! Therefore, stay free. Do not get tied up in slavery to sin again. Don't be derailed or hindered from following the truth; let the Holy Spirit guide my life as I seek Him through His Word!

2. Every day, the old man and the new man are fighting. For this reason, my "good intentions" are not enough! I know what my flesh, the old man, produces. In contrast, note how great the fruit of the Holy Spirit is! Therefore, nail the passions and evil desires of my sin nature to the Cross. Live fully in freedom.

3.

4.

NOW WHAT will I do?

1. I will bless my Savior—Jesus—for setting me free from the power and bondage of sin!

2. I will identify the person (or people) who lead me off-course or hinder me from following Jesus. Then, full of the Holy Spirit, win them for Jesus Christ.

3. I will remember the words of Billy Graham: "There are two dogs fighting inside of you. The one who wins is the one you feed!" Feed the Spirit. Starve the flesh! I will nail my sinful desires to the Cross and follow the Holy Spirit—so as to produce visible fruit *in* and *through* my life! `

4.

HERE'S WHAT I pray...

Mighty God,
thank You for sending Jesus to free me
from the bondage and penalty of sin.
I ask for more of the Holy Spirit's power
and influence in my life. Why?
Because I need Your guidance.
I need Your presence and power influencing my life.
In the name of Jesus, I pray. Amen!

Your prayer here...

ADDITIONAL NOTES

"Freedom in Christ allows you to control the desires that once controlled you."

LECRAE[11]

---

[12] As quoted at Quote Master, accessed November 18, 2021, https://www.quotemaster.org/q3cbdbf92708ce5f5e8913677a33b89de

Galatians 6:1–18

SO WHAT is God saying to me today?

1. "...If another believer is overcome by sin, you who are [spiritual] should gently and humbly help that person back onto the right path. And be careful not to fall into the same temptation yourself" (v. 1). Each day I am faced with the choice to follow the path toward spiritual life or the path toward spiritual death. Choose wisely!

2. "God is not mocked. You *will* reap what you sow!" (v.7, emphasis added) So, do not get tired of doing what is good, because at just the right moment, *I will reap a harvest of blessing if I don't give up!* (v. 9)

3.

4.

NOW WHAT will I do?

1. I will be on the "lookout" for fallen believers who need help getting back up. In addition, I will be alert and cautious so as not to fall away spiritually myself.

2. I will no longer allow my mind to compare myself to any other.

3. I will bring this sowing and reaping principle to the forefront of my thoughts (i.e. I will reap everything that I sow, both helpful *and* harmful). I will look for opportunities to do good for others, and I will not give up! The harvest of blessing is promised only to those who do not quit!

4.

5.

HERE'S WHAT I pray...

Open my eyes, God of Creation,
to look out for those who have fallen away from you
and desperately need a helping hand to get back up.
My God, please help me crucify the negative habit
of comparing myself to others.
This action is so destructive.

Please help me to sow the fruit of the Holy Spirit
so that I may reap bountiful blessings from You!
Lord, send me with Your favor to the world,
proclaiming the Good News about the Cross.
And may I be found in Your sight as a good and faithful servant. Amen!

Your prayer here...

ADDITIONAL NOTES

Ephesians

"At the timberline where the storms strike with the most fury, the sturdiest trees are found."

HUDSON TAYLOR[12]

13   As quoted at Christian Quotes, accessed November 18, 2021, https://www.christianquotes.info/quotes-by-author/hudson-taylor-quotes/

Ephesians 1:1–14

SO WHAT is God saying to me today?

1. I can only experience true peace in my life when I receive God's gifts of His mercy and grace. In Christ, God sees me as blameless! Even before He created the world, He chose me to be His. God has adopted me into His family and given me the gift of His Holy Spirit.

2. From inside a Roman prison, Paul said, "I am so blessed." Despite his less-than-ideal physical and material circumstances, Paul recognized spiritual blessing in his life. I, too, have been blessed with every spiritual blessing—not because of me or what I do, but because I belong to Jesus! Praise Him!

3.

4.

NOW WHAT will I do?

1. I offer all of my praise and deepest gratitude to the One who gave His life for me and extended the gifts of grace, peace, and His Holy Spirit! I will continue to put my trust in Jesus daily and live as a Child of God, following the guidance and direction of the Holy Spirit in my life.

2. No matter what my circumstances are in the physical and material world around me, I will look for God's spiritual blessings in my life. I will look for ways to encourage others and share with them the truth about who He is and what He has done for me.

3.

4.

HERE'S WHAT I pray...

Giver of all good gifts,
I thank You for lavishing me with Your love.
Father, thank you for choosing me before I was born
and for adopting me into Your family.
Jesus, thank you for the gift of Yourself and for salvation and forgiveness
found in You alone.
Holy Spirit, may my message always be one of encouragement
that shares this Good News with others—especially the discouraged and
depressed—so that all may know how loved they are by You.
In the name of Jesus I pray. Amen.

Your prayer here...

ADDITIONAL NOTES

"Every moment of resistance to temptation is a victory."

FREDERICK W. FABER[13]

[14] As quoted at Christian Quotes, posted December 2, 2019,
https://www.christianquotes.info/images/4-ways-to-look-at-resisting-temptation/

READ

Ephesians 1:15-23

SO WHAT is God saying to me today?

1. God's entire plan centers around Jesus Christ, who gives me an eternal inheritance of salvation, adoption, and all the blessings of Heaven! Jesus Christ purchased my freedom from sin through His blood on the cross. Because of Jesus, my sins are gone!

2. God invites me to ask for spiritual wisdom and understanding, and He offers me the same mighty power that raised Christ from the dead. Jesus is the head of the Church, and His presence and power fill all of us as members of that Body!

3.

4.

5.

NOW WHAT will I do?

1. I will remember this transformational truth when I am feeling defeated and discouraged, and I will ask for the Holy Spirit's help to walk in faith and defeat sin when it tempts me.

2. I will ask God for more spiritual wisdom and understanding. I will ask for the Spirit to fill me with the presence and power of God so that I honor and glorify Him as the Lord of my life.

3.

4.

HERE'S WHAT I pray...

My Savior and Lord,
Thank you for the gift of Yourself and the Holy Spirit living inside me.
Thank you for forgiveness and freedom from sin.
Help me walk in faith today and defeat any sin that tempts me.
Give me Your overflowing love for others,
especially the least and the lost.
I pray for spiritual wisdom and understanding.
Thank you, blessed Holy Spirit, for encouraging my heart with Your truth today.
In the name of Jesus Christ, my King. Amen.

Your prayer here...

ADDITIONAL NOTES

Ephesians 2:1–10

SO WHAT is God saying to me today?

1. Once, I was spiritually dead because of my disobedience and sin, but God changed all that by His great mercy and love when He freely gave me new life in Jesus Christ. I am now very much alive!

2. I do not deserve, nor can I earn, God's love or salvation He offers me— that is why it's by His grace that I have been saved and called righteous! By His grace and purpose upon my life, I am His masterpiece, made new in Christ Jesus; and He has planned good things for me to do on His behalf.

3.

4.

NOW WHAT will I do?

1. I will, therefore, with deepest gratitude, live my life to glorify my Savior, Jesus Christ!

2. I will listen to and obey the Holy Spirit's leading in my life. I will work to bless others and to share this Good News about the unconditional love of God with as many people as possible because...

> I was... but God!
> I used to be... but God!
> I previously lived... but God!

3.

4.

HERE'S WHAT I pray...

Merciful, loving Savior,
Thank you for Your grace poured out upon me.
Because of You, my life has meaning, purpose, and satisfaction.
I praise You.
Once dead spiritually, I am now, because of Jesus, very much alive!
Please, Lord, allow me the privilege of fulfilling Your purpose for my life
and broadcasting Your Good News to all the world.
In the name of Jesus I pray. Amen.

Your prayer here...

ADDITIONAL NOTES

Ephesians 2:11-22

SO WHAT is God saying to me today?

1. Life with Jesus is so incredibly different from life without Him! Note the contrasts:

    a.   Darkness vs. light

    b.   Distance vs. nearness

    c.   Strangers vs. citizens

    d.   Hopelessness vs. hopefulness

    e.   Division vs. unity

    f.   Death vs. life

2. The blood of Christ is the most valuable commodity in the world because it accomplishes what money, power, and fame never will. The blood of Jesus has washed away everything that separated me from God, allowing me direct access to Him.

3.

4.

NOW WHAT will I do?

1. Knowing and following Jesus brings true satisfaction and joy to my life! Therefore, I must draw close and stay close to the Lord through His Word. I will focus my time, energy, and strength on the only thing that really matters: my intimate relationship with Jesus.

2. Since much of the world lives without God (and thus without hope), I will seek opportunities to offer the hope of the Gospel to all who will receive it!

3.

4.

5.

HERE'S WHAT I pray...

Forgiving God,
Thank you for changing my life so dramatically.
You give me hope, life, and forgiveness found in no one else.
Thank you for the peace and unity of believers I experience
as part of Your family.
Help me share all of this with whomever will receive it!
I praise You, Lord Jesus.
In Your name I pray, amen.

Your prayer here...

ADDITIONAL NOTES

"I pray because I can't help myself. I pray because I'm helpless. I pray because the need flows out of me all the time, waking and sleeping. It doesn't change God. It changes me."

ANTHONY HOPKINS, AS C.S. LEWIS[14]

---

[15] *Shadowlands*, directed by Richard Attenborough (1993; UK: United International Pictures), as quoted at Essential C.S. Lewis, accessed November 17, 2021, https://essentialcslewis.com/2015/09/19/i-pray-because/

Ephesians 3:1–13

SO WHAT is God saying to me today?

1. Just as God gave Paul special responsibility to communicate His grace to others, so has God given me this opportunity. Paul was willing to go to prison for his faith because He knew God had chosen him to share this life-changing message with the world. God has chosen me, as well; may I be willing to do the same.

2. I believe God is saying to me, *I love you and I love hearing from you. Therefore, come boldly and confidently into your heavenly Father's presence. You have access to Me through faith in Christ Jesus! I will give you all you need to face every challenge and trial in your life.*

3.

4.

5.

NOW WHAT will I do?

1. I will pray for, and will be looking for, the person with whom the Lord God desires me to share His Good News of grace with today!

2. Because of my relationship with Jesus, I will speak to the Father boldly, yet with humility, asking for His help to face every challenge. Also, I will walk in a way that honors Him and brings glory to the name of Jesus, my Savior.

3.

4.

5.

HERE'S WHAT I pray...

Heavenly Father,
You alone deserve all of my praise!
I come to You in boldness and humility;
I am amazed You want to use a person like me to share Your Good News.
Please give me a strong faith like Paul
and help me honor You every day of my life,
never hesitating to share Your Good News
with those You put in my path.
In Jesus' name I pray. Amen.

Your prayer here...

ADDITIONAL NOTES

"Peace comes not from the absence of trouble, but from the presence of God."

ALEXANDER MACLAREN[15]

[16] As quoted in "In the Word—Today," posted August 17, 2021, https://inthewordtoday.com/2021/08/17/?arcf=cat:15

Ephesians 3:14-21

SO WHAT is God saying to me today?

1. Am I living in such a way, both public and private, that Jesus Christ would be "at home" in my heart and in my presence?

2. Difficulties and challenges drive us to our knees in prayer, dependence, and humility. This is what God wants from me! This is God's work within me to bring joy in the midst of life's stress, chaos, and pain.

3.

4.

5.

NOW WHAT will I do?

1. I examine myself today. I ask the question, "Is my Savior at home in my heart?" If yes, praise Him! If not, humbly repent, unlock the door to my heart, and invite Him to move in!

2. I will use life's pain, stress, and difficulties to drive me to my knees and into the Lord's presence! I will welcome the power of the Holy Spirit in my life and embrace the benefit of His presence and peace.

3.

4.

5.

HERE'S WHAT I pray...

Great God and Savior,
Thank you for making me Yours
and for working within me!
I pray that my relationship with You would be strong and enduring.
I pray that my life would visibly reflect Your presence and power in my life.
In the name of Jesus I pray. Amen.

Your prayer here...

ADDITIONAL NOTES

Ephesians 4:1–16

SO WHAT is God saying to me today?

1. I don't seek to earn God's favor; I already have it! I don't love Him so that He will love me. I love Him because He *first* loved me!

2. Because of God's love and all He's done for me, I want to honor Him with my life. As a follower of Jesus, I seek to imitate His character. Throughout the Scriptures, Jesus models for me how to be humble, gentle, and patient with others. This is the way He is with me! My life impacts others more than I realize, so I need to act as Christ's representative on earth.

3.

4.

NOW WHAT will I do?

1. I will live my life pursuing Jesus in a manner that pleases Him! How? By living with an attitude of humility, developing kindness in my speech and actions, and being patient toward others.

2. I will discover and use my spiritual gifts for the purpose of exalting God, edifying people, and sharing the Gospel with the spiritually lost.

3.

4.

HERE'S WHAT I pray...

Precious Jesus,

I love You today, not because of what You do for me, but because of who You are!

I not only want to honor and obey You, but I also want to be filled
with Your Holy Spirit.

I want to effectively use the gifts and abilities You have given me,
for the purpose of equipping the Body of Christ, to do good works for You!

Also, as Your chosen representative, help me model Your love and
character to others.

I pray this in the name of my Savior, who gave His life for me.

Amen.

Your prayer here...

ADDITIONAL NOTES

Ephesians 4:17–32

SO WHAT is God saying to me today?

1. My thoughts and attitudes about God, life, and others must be constantly changing for the better. The more I become like Jesus, the more gracious, kind, and loving I will be toward others. My specific abilities can be used to strengthen the Body of Christ. And, together with other believers, I can accomplish much more than by myself. We need each other!

2. This is solid counsel for satisfied living! Stop being mean, bad-tempered, and angry. Quarreling, harsh words, and dislike of others should have no place in my life. Instead, I will be kind, compassionate, and forgiving to others, just as God is toward me; I will "carry the banner" of peace and unity in my life.

3.

4.

NOW WHAT will I do?

1. Just as we often clean out our refrigerators, I choose to eliminate anything outdated, spoiled, or moldy in my life. This passage is crystal clear. Are you stealing? Stop! Are you lustful? Quit! Is your speech impure? Change! Is your heart holding onto bitterness and anger? Forgive now!

2. I must stay in the Word of God. Why? Because only God's Word feeds my spiritual life. Only God's Word encourages my mind and lifts my attitude. The goal of my life is not popularity but pursuit of Jesus. And the evidence of that pursuit is my continuing to change for the better!

3.

4.

5.

HERE'S WHAT I pray...

Father God, I confess and repent of the anger in my heart—
anger for not having a father to raise me;
for not having the perfect childhood;
for the burden, pain, and cost of ministry at times.
Holy Spirit, I beg You to replace my anger with joy
and contentment with what I have and for who I am.
Please bring people into my life who can help me discover
and use the abilities You have given me.
Help me to trust You and rely on Your strength
as I look for ways to encourage others.
Thank you for modeling the divine life You intended for me to live.
I pray in the name of Jesus, my Forgiver and my Savior, amen.

Your prayer here...

ADDITIONAL NOTES

*"The Bible is a flashlight for life. It illuminates
the path God has for you."*

RICK WARREN[16]

[17] As quoted on Pinterest, accessed November 18, 2021,
https://www.pinterest.com.mx/pin/368591550728516600/, likely based on:
Rick Warren, "God Gives Enough Light for the Next Step," February 10, 2017,
https://pastorrick.com/devotional/english/god-gives-enough-light-for-the-next-step/

Ephesians 5:1-16

SO WHAT is God saying to me today?

1. Just as children imitate their parents, I must imitate Jesus in all I do! It makes sense for me to follow the One who forgives, saves, and loves me! With time and through experience, I learn what pleases the Lord. When I discover it, do it without hesitation!

2. A greedy person loves and worships the temporal things of life more than he loves the eternal things of God. I must not allow our culture or the "crowd" to desensitize me from spiritual things!

3.

4.

5.

NOW WHAT will I do?

1. Because of my relationship with Jesus Christ, the way I used to live no longer dominates or controls me. These verses tell me that I *can* live differently. Out with the old, in with the new! I choose to imitate Jesus today! In the power of the Holy Spirit, I will *obey God's Word, seek His heart*, and *follow His plan* for my life.

2. In the same way I recharge my phone daily, I commit to plugging myself into God's Word daily. Without adequate power, nothing functions as designed! I will seek to discover what pleases the Lord from the Word of God. When I discover it, I will do it! I understand this is a growing process and thank God for His grace and patience with me!

3.

4.

HERE'S WHAT I pray...

Jesus, Savior of my soul and Master of my life,
I submit all that I am, and have, to You today.
I surrender my "rights," my plans, my family, and my future.
I want more of You, Jesus.
More strength. More faith. More time with You.
Please enable me to be a disciple who is making disciples!
I commit to imitating and following You like never before.
In the name of Jesus I pray, amen.

Your prayer here...

ADDITIONAL NOTES

Ephesians 5:17–33

SO WHAT is God saying to me today?

1. Be careful how I live. Be spiritually alert. Don't be tricked or blindsided. Redeem what time I have left by inviting the Lord into everything I do.

2. For me, the best marriage secret in the world is preferring my spouse to myself. The Bible says, "in humility, value others above yourself" (Philippians 2:3). Apply God's Word to my marriage and put Jesus first! If my intimacy with my spouse flows out of an intimacy with Christ, my marriage and life will be destined for success!

3.

4.

NOW WHAT will I do?

1. I invite Jesus as Lord into my life today. I surrender my thoughts and actions to Him. As Paul said to the Galatians, "I am crucified with Christ" today. May He live more and more through me each day!

2. I will live my life and my marriage in humility, valuing others above myself. I will focus my time, energy, and resources into my marriage, making my spouse my highest priority next to loving my Savior. I will actively and sacrificially love and honor her as Christ loves the Church.

3.

4.

5.

HERE'S WHAT I pray...

Lord God,
Fill me anew today with the Holy Spirit.
Open my eyes, my mind, and my heart to You.
Fill me with holiness and humility.
Help me love and honor others, especially my spouse, the way You do!
In Jesus' name I pray. Amen.

Your prayer here...

ADDITIONAL NOTES

Ephesians 6:1-9

SO WHAT is God saying to me today?

1. Instruction given to children and fathers will benefit and bless all who obey it. Therefore, I must teach my grandchildren the promises and blessings of obeying and honoring their parents.

2. Even in the mundane tasks of life, if I do them as unto the Lord, I will glorify Him and demonstrate an honoring kind of life!

3.

4.

5.

NOW WHAT will I do?

1. As a follower of Jesus, learning, obeying, and applying His Word to my life will reap benefits. I will be in the presence of Jesus daily, to feed upon His Word, be empowered by His presence, and grow in the knowledge of His grace.

2. I will do everything as if I'm doing it for God Himself—serving others with my *whole* heart, putting all of myself into my work, ministry, and even the mundane tasks of life—to honor and glorify Him!

3.

4.

HERE'S WHAT I pray...

Heavenly Father,
Thank You for providing the way to experience loving relationships.
Please help me love my family the way You love me.
Draw my grandchildren to Yourself
to obey and honor You in all of their choices.
Use me, Heavenly Father, to influence them to follow You all their days.
And help me to always serve others wholeheartedly,
honoring and glorifying You.
In Jesus' name I pray, amen.

Your prayer here...

ADDITIONAL NOTES

"Don't worry that children never listen to you, worry that they are always watching you."

ROBERT FULGHUM[17]

---

[18] As quoted at Goodreads, accessed November 12, 2021, https://www.goodreads.com/quotes/22650-don-t-worry-that-children-never-listen-to-you-worry-that

Ephesians 6:10-24

SO WHAT is God saying to me today?

1. Be strong in the Lord! We are all inundated with cultural messages telling us how to think, act, and be. Paul, however, tells us: in the Lord, and through His Word, strength will be ours. The battle belongs to God. Stand on this promise!

2. Put on the whole armor of God so that I will be prepared to fight against the forces of evil in this world. No armor is given for our backsides! God's armor is given to us to stand, fight, and face our enemy. Do not run or retreat from him!

3.

4.

5.

NOW WHAT will I do?

1.   When life is overwhelming, complicated, or hurtful, I will strengthen myself in the Lord through His Word. I will build my faith and tap into the Holy Spirit's power to stand against the influence of the evil one! Personally, when I feel down and discouraged, that is my cue to worship more, be in the Word more, serve others more.

2.   I will put on—by faith and through prayer—the whole armor of God, so that I am ready for the attacks and temptations the evil one confronts me with. After I do this, no matter what happens: stand strong.

3.

4.

HERE'S WHAT I pray...

Almighty God,
I yield myself to You alone today.
Thank you for adopting me as Your child
and giving me the gifts of Your Son and the Holy Spirit.
Put passion in my bones, steel in my resolve,
and power in my commitment to live holy and pure before You.
I put on, by faith, the armor of God today;
therefore, by Your grace and power,
I will stand *for* You and *with* You no matter what!
Please make me thirsty and hungry for more of You
and Your Word, each day.
In Jesus' name I pray, amen.

Your prayer here...

ADDITIONAL NOTES

"Faith is not simply a patience that passively suffers until the storm is past. Rather, it is a spirit that bears things—with resignations, yes, but above all, with blazing, serene hope."

CORAZON AQUINO[18]

19 As quoted at Brainy Quote, accessed November 12, 2021,
    https://www.brainyquote.com/quotes/corazon_aquino_201108,

Helpful Resources

1. www.gotquestions.org
   Galatians: The NIV Application Commentary by Scot McKnight

2. www.blueletterbible.com

3. *Begin: A Journey Through Scriptures for Seekers and New Believers* by Ken Ham and Bodie Hodge

4. *Life Application Study Bible,* New Living Translation

5. *The Living Bible*

6. www.bibleproject.com

Author Bio

MIKE SILVA is an individual—with a passionate calling—sent out on a mission to promote and communicate the life-changing message of Jesus Christ.

Mike lost his father in a tragic car accident when he was six years old. He battled for years with anger, bitterness, and blaming God for his loss... struggling to find purpose in his pain. Finally, he discovered—in his Heavenly Father—the unending love, forgiveness, comfort, hope, and peace he longed for when he accepted Christ as his personal Savior. By the time he was 19, the Lord had clearly called him to do the work of an evangelist and to share Jesus with the nations.

For more than 40 years, Silva has proclaimed the Gospel face-to-face with millions of people in dozens of nations throughout the world.

Silva believes "growling stomachs have deaf ears"[19]; therefore, his team aims to meet both spiritual and physical needs. As a result, thousands of families have received food, clothing, medical care, and clean water through their compassion aid ministry.

Mike has been married to his beautiful wife, Crystal, for over four decades. Together they have been blessed with four wonderful daughters, sons-in-law, and grandchildren.

You can find Mike on Facebook, Instagram, Twitter, YouTube, and at: www.mikesilva.org/ and www.festivalporlavida.com/global/.

---

[20] Spoken to Mike by a pastor in Nigeria years ago.

Mission Statement

...to Practice and Proclaim the life-changing message of the Lord Jesus Christ in the world's most spiritually receptive places."

Share Your Story with Us!

MIKE SILVA
INTERNATIONAL

The greatest incentive for prayer is answered prayer!

So, I want to hear from you!

How has the Lord answered your prayers?

Please share with me, and with your permission, I will share with others.